Original title:
Life's Purpose: To Keep You Guessing

Copyright © 2025 Creative Arts Management OÜ
All rights reserved.

Author: Miriam Kensington
ISBN HARDBACK: 978-1-80566-044-6
ISBN PAPERBACK: 978-1-80566-339-3

Whispers of the Unknown

In an echo of socks, lost and found,
A treasure chest of silly sounds.
The fridge hums secrets at midnight's peak,
Why do ducks quack? We can only sneak.

Fate plays tricks like a playful cat,
Swirling stories in a top hat.
Jellybeans dance on the candy shelf,
While I search for the meaning of myself.

The Game of Possibilities

Life's a game of dice and chance,
Where turtles take a wobbly stance.
Pick a card, any card, it says,
Watch a snail win in a messy maze.

Banana peels grant the best slips,
Who knew fate's got such funny quips?
With every turn, surprise awaits,
Like a clown hiding behind the gates.

Serendipity's Riddle

A llama in a tutu prances by,
As muffins debate if they can fly.
The toaster sings as bread turns gold,
Tales of wonder quietly unfold.

In the café of fate, spills are dreams,
Cups clink laughter; nothing's as it seems.
Should I wear polka dots or stripes?
Decisions hide in playful gripes.

Chasing the Elusive Dream

A dream bounced high on rubber feet,
It giggles, dances, skips down the street.
Chasing it feels like a wild chase,
As jelly-cats lead a silly race.

With marshmallow clouds and candy rain,
Each step's a giggle, yet brings some pain.
What's waiting at the end of the line?
Is it pizza or maybe just wine?

Glimmers in the Fog

Amidst the shrouded morning haze,
A squirrel ponders, lost in a maze.
He chases shadows, thinks it's fate,
But finds a nut that's way too late.

A bird that claims he's learned it all,
Trips on a twig, begins to fall.
He flaps his wings and calls it art,
While landing soft on gardener's heart.

A fish debates the ocean's rules,
Swimming through schools, just being fools.
He dreams of flying, oh what a plight,
While splashing clouds that won't take flight.

So here we dance in quirks sublime,
With every stutter, we find our rhyme.
In this great circus, we laugh and play,
Forever guessing, come what may.

The Wonder of Untamed Paths

A child of wonder, shoes untied,
Explores the world, with eyes opened wide.
Each twist and turn, a new surprise,
As muddy frogs wear disguises.

A cat in boots, with dreams so grand,
Plans an adventure to foreign land.
He maps it out, but loses track,
Then nibbles cheese from the knapsack.

An old wise turtle, slow yet bold,
Keeps secrets of paths that turn to gold.
He chuckles softly, saying, "Oh dear!
The fun is found when you veer from here!"

As stars align in chaotic swirl,
We trip on paths and give a twirl.
With giggles echoing amidst the fun,
What's lost is laughter, never done.

The Symphony of Unanswered Questions

In a world of curious plots,
Where answers dance and skip,
We ponder why we buy blue socks,
While still avoiding ships.

With riddles wrapped in silly jokes,
And puzzles made of yarn,
We laugh as life shifts like a Jester,
With clowns that never learn.

The cat is chasing shadows now,
While we just scratch our heads,
And wonder why the sky is blue,
While comfort lies in beds.

Oh, life is quite a mismatch game,
With pieces hard to find,
Yet every twist just makes us smile,
It's fun, you'll find it kind.

Veiled in Mystery

Behind the curtains of the day,
The questions pop like corn,
Why is the chicken on the road?
To dodge the kids with scorn.

The ice cream melts in summer's rays,
With sprinkles lost in time,
Yet still we search for answers bright,
Amidst the silly rhyme.

Our thoughts like balloons float away,
Deflated by the night,
We chase the whims of fleeting dreams,
They vanish out of sight.

So let's embrace the wobbly truth,
And paint it with a grin,
For mystery is just so funny,
Let the guessing begin!

The Enigma of Now

Here's a riddle, I declare,
Why do socks always hide?
In the drawers of forgotten lands,
Where mismatched dreams abide.

We watch the clock tick-tock along,
With seconds dressed in flair,
But seconds are a bit like cats,
They're sneaky, I declare.

A sandwich sings a silent tune,
While voices hum in pairs,
And whispers wrap around our thoughts,
In comical affairs.

Let's dance in circles, spin around,
With giggles on our trail,
For questions spark a merry game,
Where laughter will prevail.

Footsteps on an Undefined Path

I took a stroll on paths unknown,
With shoes that squeaked just right,
Each step a question in my head,
Why don't ducks wear tights?

The trees they whisper tales of yore,
Their leaves a rustling cheer,
But all we hear are echoes bold,
Of things we aren't so clear.

With every choice, a fork appears,
Like spaghetti on the floor,
We laugh and choose the wobbly way,
While craving a bit more.

So let's embrace the winding road,
With giggles at each bend,
For every laugh a mystery brought,
Is one more silly friend.

Curves in the Road

I once took a turn, oh what a delight,
But ended up lost, in the middle of night.
The GPS laughed, said, "You're quite the bold,
Chasing after answers, but it's all on hold."

A sign read 'Detour', I grinned at the fun,
With each twist and turn, the journey's begun.
The road was a riddle, but I found my way,
In the chaos of twists, I twirled like a ballet.

The Mystery of Each Step

I walked down the street, shoes on the wrong feet,
Each step was a gamble, with my own heartbeat.
I tripped over thoughts, did a dance with a cat,
  Life's little tricks, always hide and chat.

A puddle appeared, did I jump or did splash?
My shoes now all soggy, but isn't that a blast?
The sidewalk was winking, 'You'll never know more',
With every misstep, there's a new door to explore.

Truths Beneath the Surface

I dug in my garden, seeking pearls of might,
Found a worm laughing, in the broad daylight.
"Dig deeper," it said, "for treasures so rare,
But watch out for roots, they'll give you a scare!"

I unearthed a boot, now isn't that neat?
With a note inside saying "I once had two feet!"
The truths that we seek may make us just grin,
For often it's nonsense that hides in within.

The Puzzle of Existence

I bought a puzzle, the box said 'complete',
But missing was corner, what a sneaky feat!
Piece after piece, I sorted with flair,
Only to find a cat stealing the square.

Each fragment a laugh, twisting in the light,
Life's quirky design, making wrong feel right.
I ponder the picture, it shifts like the sun,
The fun's in the chaos, so let's not be done!

Fables of the Future

In the land of what might be,
The cows wear hats, sipping tea.
Flying pigs paint the skies,
While clocks run backward with sighs.

A squirrel dons a bright blue tie,
He negotiates with birds that fly.
Dancing trees have witty chats,
As sunflowers wear quirky hats.

Here, the grass grows up to dance,
As kittens twirl in a silly prance.
A wizard lost his spellbook too,
He long forgot just what to do.

In this realm, the wild absurd,
Each twist is thus a playful word.
Who knows what tomorrow brings?
Maybe a frog with golden wings?

The Spiral of Intentions

Round and round the hamster spins,
Debates with goldfish — who wins?
Their audience, a cat named Wally,
Issues a challenge — a grand rally!

The cheese is rolling down the path,
Creating laughter, causing wrath.
Pizza clouds float high and free,
While dinosaurs sip iced fern tea.

A joke's a riddle without a clue,
Spinning life's wheel—what will it do?
Marshmallows bounce on trampoline seams,
While unicorns plot impossible dreams.

Intentions twisted like pretzel knots,
Leave everyone guessing, in funny spots.
Whims of fate with a playful dance,
Make living feel just like a prance.

Mirrors of Reflection

Look in the mirror, what do you see?
A wacky version of you, oh me!
A nose of a clown, the ears of a mouse,
Trying to fit in, this mirror's a house.

Reflections giggle and wink back with glee,
A cloudy day feels like a sunny spree.
When you smile wide, the mirror does too,
It knows all the secrets, yet keeps them askew.

Here the truth plays hide and seek,
Do you dare peek into the mystique?
Lions laugh in the glass with pride,
In a world that's both silly and wide.

What do we learn from such mirrors round?
That laughter in chaos is easily found.
With reflections that twist and turn about,
Let's embrace the laughs and not the doubt.

Unwritten Blueprints

Sketching dreams on napkins bright,
Plans get lost by morning light.
A cat chooses to be the chief,
While the printer runs out of relief.

Designs on coffee cups all swirl,
Each idea makes a funny twirl.
Lego bricks, a castle now,
Were supposed to be a peaceful cow!

Blueprints dance with silly flair,
Doodles everywhere, without a care.
The architect forgot his scale,
And drew a dragon, mixing detail!

In the end, we build by chance,
With mismatched socks leading the dance.
So join the chaos, laugh out loud,
In unwritten tales, we are all proud.

The Mirage of Clarity

In a world that spins like a top,
We seek answers, but they just hop.
The clearer the path, the more we stray,
Like a cat chasing light, in disarray.

Questions parade in a silly march,
With answers hiding under the arch.
Why did the chicken cross the street?
To avoid the riddles on repeat!

Like a treasure map with no 'X' in sight,
We wander blindly, what a funny plight.
We laugh at the questions that keep arising,
Maybe the chaos is just surprising!

So dance with the questions, don't despair,
In this game of life, just don't beware.
Clarity is a mirage far away,
Let's embrace the confusion and laugh all day!

A Canvas Yet to Be Painted

With brushes in hand, we start to play,
But colors mix in the silliest way.
What shade is joy? Is it green or blue?
I dipped in both and ended up with goo!

Life's canvas is blank, or so they say,
But doodles and scribbles just seem to stray.
A masterpiece? More like a funny jest,
Each stroke a giggle, each color a quest.

Palette of dreams, wild and bright,
We paint in circles, what a sight!
A splash of chaos, a dash of cheer,
Who knew confusion could be so dear?

So let the canvas lead on the way,
Trust the process; it's here to play.
In every mistake a gem you'll find,
Just laugh it off, and don't be blind!

The Dance of Uncertainty

Step left, step right, a twist, a whirl,
In the dance of doubt, watch the feet twirl.
Is it a tango or is it a jig?
Whichever it is, it's big and vague!

Partners change in this quirky dance,
With uncertainty leading, who gets a chance?
Spinning in circles, on toes we go,
Is that your left, or did I miss the show?

The music is strange, yet we start to sway,
With laughter and stumbles, we find our way.
Sometimes we fall, often we rise,
In this dance of life, we improvise!

So grab a partner, join in the fun,
No lesson planned, just let it run.
In each awkward move, let joy ignite,
In the dance of the uncertain, we all unite!

The Twist in the Tale

Once upon a time, the story began,
With a hero so bold, a brave little man.
But wait, what's this? A twist in the plot,
Our hero's a chicken! Oh, what a thought!

Quest for the treasure? Or maybe a snack?
Journey through jungles with no way back.
Spotted a dragon, but alas, it's a cat,
With whiskers and purrs, oh, how about that?

Adventure awaits in the pages we make,
With laughter and giggles, let's not forsake.
In every turn, a chuckle we find,
For the twist in the tale tickles the mind!

So grab your pen and let stories unfold,
With winks and pranks, let the silliness mold.
In each little twist, an adventure we hail,
For the joy is in riding the curious trail!

The Tapestry of Transformation

Every day starts unique, it seems,
Like socks that hide in laundering schemes.
We rise with plans, all neat in a row,
Then chaos knocks, and off we go!

Coffee spills like a wild fountain,
The cat's in charge; he's king of the mountain.
We chase our dreams in odd little ways,
Misplacing our keys for days and days!

But laughter rings loud in the mess we make,
With each little blunder, we grow and shake.
So dance in the rain, with all of your might,
Transforming the day into pure delight!

Secrets Lurking in Everyday Moments

Beneath the routine, oh, what a find,
A treasure of quirks and funnies entwined.
A sandwich that giggles, a cat that pretends,
To plot world domination with all of his friends!

The mailbox chuckles as bills come its way,
It's a comedy club in the light of the day.
A sneeze like a trumpet brings laughter, not dread,
While crumbs of joy dance on crumbs of bread!

Every moment a puzzle, a riddle to tease,
With snacks that conspire to make us unease.
So savor the odd, let your worries unfurl,
In this circus of quirks, we give life a whirl!

The Riddle of Light and Shadow

In shadows that play on the wall, they say,
Lies the secret of life, in a whimsical way.
A flickering bulb with a mind of its own,
Turns night into laughter, in a wild over-tone!

The sun slaps the pavement, it giggles a lot,
While clouds play hide-and-seek, oh what a plot!
Light dances with shadows, it's quite a charade,
As the kitten chases both, thinking it's made!

Each twist and turn brings a twist of fate,
As we trip on our dreams, feeling rather great.
So stay on this ride, with a wink and a grin,
For light and dark play, their game begins!

A Journey Without a Map

We wander and ponder, with snacks in our pack,
Maps are for normal folks, that's a fact!
With GPS blinking, we drive 'round and round,
While mystery shops pop up without sound!

Oh look, a llama at a gas station stop,
Who knew that this journey would never quite drop?
Lost in the giggles, we find our own path,
As fate serves up laughter, and math takes a bath!

So let's toss the directions, let's have some fun,
With twists and turns, we still haven't done.
Adventure awaits in our hearts, what a map!
Let's toast to the wild, and eek out a clap!

Pathways to the Unseen

Why does the squirrel steal my shoe?
Is it a game or just for the view?
Underneath the moon's soft gleam,
I wonder if I'll ever deem.

A pizza topped with chocolate chips,
Might lead to some unusual trips.
The paths we take are quite absurd,
Like chatting with a talking bird.

The cat thinks she knows it all,
As she plans her next great fall.
We dance between the known and strange,
In this merry world, so full of change.

The Art of Curious Living

A pickle jar that's stuck so tight,
Is my arm strong enough to fight?
Life's a puzzle, quirky and bold,
With pieces scattered, stories untold.

Floating on a rubber duck,
I ponder if I've run out of luck.
Each twist and turn is off the wall,
Chasing shadows that giggle and call.

I think I saw my socks take flight,
In a disco ball of pure delight.
The dances we do, oh what a sight!
Living curious, all day and night.

Secrets of the Turning Seasons

Autumn leaves are whispering loud,
As if they've gathered quite a crowd.
They tell of summer's secret dreams,
And winter's plans for icy schemes.

A snowman wearing flip-flops bright,
Questions whether it's day or night.
Springtime blooms in polka dots,
While summer wears a hundred spots.

Nature's laugh is quite the show,
With every twist, it steals the glow.
In every season's playful tease,
Life grows curious with utmost ease.

Riddles Woven in Time

Clocks are ticking a riddle loud,
As if they're wearing a laughing shroud.
How many ticks till I find me?
Or will I just sip warm chamomile tea?

The toaster pops with toast so high,
Did I just hear it say goodbye?
Jellybeans roll on the floor,
As I ponder what they're really for.

In the garden, gnomes shake hands,
As the light of day quietly expands.
With every riddle, the sun will climb,
Forever dancing with sweetened rhyme.

Beyond the Veil of Certainty

In a world where answers hide,
We seek the truth, but there's no guide.
Like socks that vanish in the wash,
We chase the meaning, yet feel posh.

A cat that speaks would keep us wise,
But all we get are furtive sighs.
We juggle dreams like clumsy clowns,
While wisdom wears mismatched crowns.

A dance we do, on life's grand stage,
With scripts that rewrite on each page.
We trip on secrets, slip on fate,
And laugh along at how we plate.

So here's a toast, let's raise our cup,
To the silly things that fill us up.
For in the jest, we find our way,
In not-knowing, we love to play.

A Journey Through the Unknown

With a map that's drawn in crayon bright,
We venture forth into the night.
A compass spins; it's lost its mind,
Yet off we go, no need to find.

Like detectives chasing ghosts of dreams,
We wander through the wildest schemes.
Each twist and turn a laughable oops,
We wear our mishaps like silly loops.

The road ahead is fogged with fun,
We'll take the path less traveled, run!
With every bump, a chuckle blooms,
And joy erupts in strange cartoons.

So grab a snack and join the ride,
In this bizarre and silly stride.
The journey's what we came to see,
As questions pop like bubbles, whee!

The Puzzle of Existence

A jigsaw missing half the parts,
Pieces scattered, like our hearts.
We search for meaning in the mess,
But laughter pulls us from distress.

A riddle wrapped in mismatched socks,
Our thoughts are tangled, like old clocks.
What's the answer? Who could know?
We giggle as we steal the show.

The pieces fit, then shift and sway,
Like dancing specters in dismay.
We ponder deep with every crack,
While our brains are stuck, just bring a snack.

In the chaos, humor thrives,
It's here we find our silliest drives.
So let's embrace the jumbled scene,
In this puzzle, we reign supreme!

Serendipity's Hidden Map

A treasure hunt without a clue,
The X marks spots where dreams come true.
But wait, is that a raccoon's lair?
Or just our hopes tangled in hair?

Each twist and turn brings mad surprise,
With maps designed by eager spies.
A twist of fate, like silly strings,
The kind that pulls and often stings.

So follow trails paved with delight,
As whimsical as a chicken fight.
For serendipity loves to tease,
And wraps us in her gentle breeze.

So here we are, lost but not blue,
On roads that lead us to the zoo.
With laughter guiding every step,
The hidden map is ours, adept!

The Allure of Hidden Doors

Behind closed doors, what do we find?
A cat in a hat or a jug of wind?
Mysteries swirl with a giggle or sigh,
Next thing we know, it's a pie in the sky.

What's on the other side, a treasure or foe?
Just a squirrel in a tux, putting on a show.
Every twist and turn tickles the brain,
For what is the point of this zany game?

Sometimes there's joy in the paths we forsake,
Like candy for breakfast, or pies made of cake.
So open that door, take the leap and peek,
In the world of surprises, it's fun to be meek.

A dance with the absurd, a chuckle or two,
In the chaos of choices, who's keeping the cue?
A jest in the hallway, a prank in the light,
So we spin through the day, making wrong feel quite right.

The Unseen Weavings of Fate

Threads of the unseen, tangled and bright,
We weave through the days, wrapped up in delight.
A wink from the cosmos, a laugh from the stars,
Even socks in the dryer are rearranged with bars.

What's coming next? A dance or a fall?
Perhaps a grand feast, or just crumbs on the wall.
A twist of the yarn, a knot in the thread,
Hilarity reigns in the paths that we tread.

With each little misstep, we giggle in glee,
'Cause who knows what fate has planned, can we see?
A fortune cookie breaks, proclaiming a prize,
Only to find it's a cupcake in disguise.

So let's frolic through time, with laughter and cheer,
The unseen weavings, let's not take too near.
For in every odd twist, there's laughter to stake,
And a life full of joy is the grandest mistake.

The Twilight of Knowing

In the twilight of knowing, what can we claim?
A riddle wrapped tightly, like a joke or a game.
There's wisdom in folly, it seems to unfold,
Like a chicken that crosses just to be bold.

Questions like bubbles, shimmering bright,
Float in confusion, and dance in the night.
What's true and what isn't? The line starts to blur,
As we fish for the answers, just feel the warm purr.

So let's wade through the murk, take a jolly old guess,
And turn the unknown into a playful mess.
Maybe the truth is a pie for the eyes,
Or a quirky old tale with fantastic surprise.

In the twilight of guessing, we find joy that it brings,
With laughter and wonder, oh, the chaos it flings!
For in knowing too much, we might just get stuck,
Instead, let's embrace it, like a dog chasing luck.

The Curiosity That Drives Us

Oh, what really drives us, this thirst that we hold?
A question, a query, or maybe pure gold?
Like cats chasing lasers, with eyes all aglow,
We dive into chaos, unsure where to go.

Curiosity tickles, it dances and plays,
Finding magic in moments, in oh-so-strange ways.
A sock in the fridge, or a hat on a cat,
We chuckle and ponder, let's have a chat.

With a keen sense of wonder, we open the door,
To a circus of thoughts, a whimsical score.
Every twist and stumble, a laugh to bestow,
In the light of our questions, we wiggle and flow.

So let's ride the wild waves, this curious tide,
With jokes as our lifeboat, and giggles as guide.
For life is a puzzle wrapped tightly in cheer,
With the curiosity that drives us, there's nothing to fear!

The Unknown Canvas

A blank page waits with eager eyes,
Colors dance in wild surprise.
With each brush, a twist or turn,
Creating art as candles burn.

Whispers hint at dreams untold,
While clumsy strokes turn shy and bold.
Expect the giggles, brace for gasps,
As the canvas, it clasps.

Splashes here and dribbles there,
A masterpiece of joyful flair.
Who knew that purple llamas roam?
On this canvas, I find home.

So paint your heart and just let go,
The art of fun is what we know.
In every splotch, a story blooms,
Amid the laughter, chaos looms.

Between Questions and Answers

Why did the chicken cross the road?
Was it for laughter, or some hidden code?
Between the queries, a comedic tune,
Answers flit away like a balloon.

Here's a riddle, here's a jest,
The more we ponder, the less we rest.
As questions pile, a mountain high,
We giggle at mysteries like a pie in the sky.

Life's perplexing, oh what a ride!
With each new answer, confusion will glide.
We scratch our heads, we laugh, we sigh,
Between the doubts, we all get by.

So let's raise a toast to the unknown,
For in the chaos, our laughter has grown.
Bring on the questions, let's dance and play,
In this riddle fest, we'll find our way.

The Whirlwind of Whims

In a tornado of bright, silly dreams,
Where giggles echo and sunlight beams.
A waltz with whims, how sweetly we spin,
Round and round, let the fun begin.

What's next, a trampoline or a joke?
Perhaps a gentle breeze or a puff of smoke?
Each twist and turn a surprise out loud,
In this whirlwind, we laugh so proud.

Balloons that float on a rainy day,
Chasing shadows in a comical way.
Our hearts take flight, just like a kite,
In the whirlwind of whims, all feels right.

So come join the dance, leave cares behind,
Follow the laughter that's sweet, unconfined.
In this joyful storm, our voices soar,
Embracing the whims forevermore.

A Tangle of Hopes

In a garden of dreams, wild hope abounds,
Tangled vines make curious sounds.
A daisy wishes on a star at night,
While marigolds giggle, oh what a sight!

Who tied these strings? It's quite absurd,
Each loop and knot tells a funny word.
One moment, a climb, the next, a fall,
In this tangle of hopes, we embrace it all.

A wink from fate, a slip on a shoe,
The garden of dreams is never quite blue.
With laughter as sunshine, let's plant a few,
And watch as our hopes take flight and renew.

So hold dear your dreams, let them interlace,
For in this tangle, we find our place.
With smiles and giggles, together we'll roam,
In the mess of it all, we feel right at home.

Breaths Between Moments

In the chaos of a bustling day,
I lost my socks; they ran away!
Cup of coffee in a lovely haze,
Or was it tea? I'm in a daze.

I thought I'd find my purpose clear,
But instead, I found a missing steer.
Chasing dreams on roller skates,
Just hoping they won't roll in fates.

The sun forgot to start the show,
And clouds decided not to glow.
I packed my bags, or was it lunch?
Are we on pause, or did I punch?

So here we are, a wobbly cheer,
For all the laughs that disappear.
With every twist and silly turns,
We embrace the fun, for that's what burns.

Unraveled Threads of Tomorrow

I knitted dreams with yarns so bright,
But tangled up before the night.
I thought I'd map my every path,
Instead, I found a monster's wrath.

The future's stash is full of quirks,
Like socks with stripes that come in jerks.
Should I choose the hat or shoe?
My calendar's a puzzle too!

I tried to play the wise old sage,
But tripped and fell on this fine stage.
The curtain's up, the actors flee,
And I'm just laughing at the spree.

Each little plan is a magic spell,
That turns out funky, can't you tell?
The threads unravel, but I won't frown,
For every twist brings a cheerful crown.

Whispers in the Cosmic Dance

In starlit skies, I danced with glee,
But tripped on meteors, oh woe is me!
Galaxies twirl with snacks in hand,
While I just hope to understand.

The cosmos chuckles, stars align,
While I search for that last slice of pie.
Planets gossip, and I'm just here,
Confused if I should laugh or cheer.

Uranus giggles, with a sly little wink,
And Saturn spins with a clink.
I tried to follow the comet's flight,
But landed flat, what a silly sight!

In this vast space, oh what a jest,
Where nothing fits and all's a test.
We twirl and spin, a cosmic chance,
As life just giggles at the dance.

The Labyrinth Within

I wandered deep inside my mind,
Where puzzles wait, and snacks are kind.
With every turn, I lose my keys,
But find old nibbles of memories.

The walls are painted with strange faces,
And every door leads to weird places.
I tried to map this silly maze,
But got distracted by a haze.

A talking cat gives tips with flair,
While juggling birds float in the air.
I asked him where the exit lies,
He chuckled loud and said, "Surprise!"

Embrace the twirls, don't take the bait,
In this wild world, it's never late.
With laughter echoing through the walls,
We'll wade through whimsy as fun enthralls.

Echoes of Uncertainty

In the morning I wear socks,
But they never find their pairs.
My toaster's a timid ghost,
It only speaks through stares.

The cat judges my every move,
Like I'm a circus clown.
What's the use of a plan,
When it's wrapped in a frown?

Beneath the bed the dust bunnies play,
Holding meetings at three.
I've got to know how they vote,
Do they pick Cat or me?

Why do I talk to my plants?
Do they find me amusing?
In the garden of doubts I roam,
Where questions are confusing.

The Dance of Endless Whys

Why is the sky blue today?
Did the clouds have a meeting?
And why does my lunch run away,
When I'm sure it was greeting?

The fridge hums a tuneful song,
As leftovers start to dance.
I think they want to tag along,
For a fridge-inspired romance.

Do socks plot my ultimate doom,
When they vanish out of sight?
My closet must hold a secret room,
Where lost items laugh at night.

If life's a big pie, who gets a slice?
Are the crumbs just for fun?
I'm just here to roll the dice,
And play 'who's won, who's done?'

Shadows of Tomorrow

Shadows stretch, wiggle, and sway,
Making faces at me.
They whisper secrets from the day,
Or is it just wishful glee?

The future wears a quirky hat,
With feathers, bright and loud.
It floats by on a rubber mat,
Drawing in a whimsical crowd.

Why do I trip over my dreams?
They're supposed to lift me high!
But they tumble like playful streams,
And splash mud in my eye.

The calendar throws a wild party,
Events lost in a whirl.
I'll just follow the trail of confetti,
With a grin and a twirl.

Pathways in the Dark

I wander through the shadows long,
With a flashlight and a snack.
My only guide is a whimsical song,
Sung by the squirrels in black.

What's lurking behind the tree?
Perhaps it's just a breeze.
Or maybe a mystery critter,
Telling jokes with perfect ease.

The path ahead twists and turns,
Each corner holds surprise.
With giggles, my uncertainty burns,
Like fireflies in the skies.

So I trot like a clumsy deer,
In a twilight of make-believe.
Every step brings me a cheer,
Even the dark has tricks up its sleeve.

The Canvas of Questions

A canvas wide, all colors blend,
Each stroke a query, round the bend.
Why's the sky blue, or do fish sing?
Grab your brush, it's a puzzling thing.

With splashes bold, and dabs of doubt,
Here's a riddle we can't live without.
Do cows dance when the moon is bright?
Or do they just moo in the dead of night?

What's the secret to a perfect pie?
Perhaps it's sprinkles that reach the sky.
Could socks hide treasures, don't ask me how?
Might bees wear hats, do they take a bow?

In this mad art, we draw and jest,
Finding answers is just like a quest.
So paint your life, with giggles and cheer,
Embrace the wild questions that appear!

Secrets in the Shadows

In darkness lurk, the mysteries played,
Why does your toast always fall buttered?
What's hiding behind the fridge's door?
Did you lose your keys, or are they on tour?

Scooby-Doo has nothing on these tales,
Ghostly giggles and bizarre trails.
Why do the socks vanish, never to return?
Are they plotting, or do they simply yearn?

Where's that sock you wore in June?
Is it a secret or just a cartoon?
With shadows dancing, we navigate tight,
Laughing alone in the corner at night.

Unearth the laughs in moments bizarre,
Like wondering who stashed your chocolate bar!
So, tiptoe softly, through mirthful decay,
Finding secrets that make us sway!

Beyond the Horizon of Certainty

A ship sets sail on a sea of doubt,
With waves of wonder and whims that flout.
Is the horizon really where dreams end?
Or a trick of the light that loves to pretend?

Are stars just holes in the cosmic quilt?
Or whispers of wishes, gracefully built?
Navigating riddles like a clumsy dance,
Do fish wear glasses, or take a chance?

With every wave, a giggle emerges,
As we ponder life's curious surges.
What's the password to the universe?
A pun? A joke? Or a crazy verse?

Set your sails to catch the breeze of whim,
In the unpredictable, let your spirit swim.
For beyond each bow, with laughter and jest,
Are treasures unknown, and mysteries blessed!

Labyrinth of Choices

A maze of paths, with twists and turns,
Should I eat cake or take up concerns?
Do I wear shoes, or dance in the rain?
Will I solve it, or go quite insane?

Left or right, which way to go?
Is that a chicken, or your neighbor Joe?
Pick a door, and hear that noise,
Is it laughter or just little boys?

With humor as our guiding light,
Shall we chase down flights in the night?
Do we leap over puddles, or jump on the train?
Choices abound, let's go quite insane!

In this labyrinth, we stumble and fall,
Finding joy in the slip and the crawl.
So choose your adventure, let giggles arise,
For in every choice, there's a quirky surprise!

The Tapestry of What If

In a world of tangled choices,
We dance on threads of fate,
What if unicorns wore shoes?
Now that would be first-rate!

Should I wear a hat or not?
Maybe flip-flops in the snow?
When socks escape to hidden spots,
Who really knows where they go?

What if pizza flew around?
With toppings as the sky,
Each slice a gust of flavor,
Turning bland days spry!

Shall I juggle orange juice?
Or ride a llama through the park?
In the tapestry of whims,
The laughter leaves its mark!

Threads of Wonder

Every thread a tale to tell,
Woven through my mind,
What if squirrels ran for office?
Would they be kind or blind?

Coffee beans that dance at night,
With sugar as their beat,
What if chairs could shout and sing?
This rhythm could be sweet!

A world where cats teach yoga,
And dogs are baristas too,
What if my goldfish can conquer?
The hoopla of a zoo!

With every twist and turn I take,
In threads of wonder spun,
The quirky paths are beckoning,
Oh, how can this be fun?

Echoing Footprints

Footprints in the sand, they say,
Are left by folks who roam,
What if they were giant clowns?
Would that feel like home?

Two left shoes and mismatched socks,
Are symbols of my quest,
What if penguins wore sunglasses?
I'd take that as a jest!

Echoing through silly pathways,
Laughter fills the air,
What if jellybeans could talk?
Their stories do declare!

In the dance of strange questions,
With each step that I take,
Echoes of the weirdest thoughts
Create a fun mistake!

The Art of Wandering

With a map that leads to nowhere,
I wander on a whim,
What if tacos could do ballet?
Oh, life is quite a hymn!

Should I stop and wave to clouds?
Or challenge squirrels to a race?
What if trees could blow a kiss?
Would that be a silly face?

The art of roaming freely here,
Is filled with every grin,
What if rainbows had a flavor?
And tasted like a spin!

In the chaos of my journey,
Each twist a giggling plight,
The art of wandering says this:
Just stay absurdly light!

Beneath the Surface of Still Waters

In calm lakes where reflections play,
Fish plot their mischief, come what may.
Bubbles rise, secrets they hold,
While ducks quack tales, both daring and bold.

The pond is quiet, but don't be misled,
A turtle bets on who'll lose their head.
A frog leaps high, aiming for flies,
While wise old fish roll their big fishy eyes.

Under the stillness, chaos can brew,
A swirl of laughter, a joke or two.
For every calm, there's a laugh yet unseen,
Beneath the surface, life's a silly routine.

So join in the giggles, embrace the surprise,
As ripples of humor dance 'neath the skies.
With each splash, wisdom we find,
In the murky depths of a whimsical mind.

Infinite Turns and Twists

Life's a maze of winding lanes,
With funny signs and baffling gains.
Every turn leads to a new surprise,
Like running into the neighbor's prize.

Around the corner, a cat gives chase,
While dogs just laugh at the human race.
A snail competes; oh, what a sight!
Who knew slow could be the fastest flight?

You switch the light and the shadows play,
Squirrels dance like they own the day.
Each twist you take might muffle your cheer,
But unexpected giggles always draw near.

Embrace the chaos, enjoy the spins,
For in each false start, the comedy begins.
So grab your map, or toss it away,
Let the whims guide you through laughter's bouquet.

The Dance of Possibilities

In every hour, a chance unfolds,
A dance of stories yet untold.
Every step a riddle, a playful tease,
As socks go missing, just like your keys.

The music shifts, you twirl and sway,
Why did the chicken cross? Who knows, hey?
With every fail, you perfect a move,
Life's silly jigs always manage to groove.

With jazz hands flying, mistakes become art,
You trip over feet, but that's just the start.
Laughter echoes with every misstep,
These are the moments, so brimming with pep.

So tiptoe lightly, or stomp with delight,
As possibilities whirl in the soft moonlight.
For amidst the stumble, you'll surely find,
The best partners are those with a whimsical mind.

Lanterns in the Dark

In the night where fears often creep,
A glow from lanterns starts to peep.
They flicker and dance, making shadows play,
While jokes float about—hilarious ballet.

You stumble on laughter, trip on a tale,
As whispers of mischief set hangers to sail.
Ghosts hiding behind, in hilarious fright,
Play peek-a-boo 'til the first morning light.

Sparkly ideas drift like fireflies,
Witty banter ignites the skies.
Each lantern a dream, each light a jest,
Filling the dark with humorous zest.

So gather round, let's light up the way,
With chuckles and smiles that forever stay.
For in the shadows, laughter will spark,
Guiding our hearts like lanterns in the dark.

Threads of Enigma

In a world of whimsy, we all play along,
With riddles and puzzles, we can't help but throng.
A cat with a hat, no clue what's in store,
Like juggling jellybeans, who could ask for more?

The sun winks at shadows, a quirky ballet,
While clocks tick backward, leading us astray.
Bananas in pajamas dance on a wire,
Unraveling nonsense, but oh, the desire!

Every twist and turn, we giggle and spin,
Chasing our tails like the world's best of twins.
A map with no X, directions all blurred,
The joy in the chaos, the best kind of word!

So here's to the whims that gently redirect,
To silly surprises, and all we suspect.
For in every question, a mystery lies,
With laughter and wonder, we'll open our eyes.

In Pursuit of Fleeting Dreams

I chased a wild dream on a pogo stick,
It bounced through the clouds, oh what a trick!
With marshmallow mountains and rivers of cream,
I laughed as I stumbled, lost in the dream.

A rabbit in sneakers, he darts and he weaves,
Telling me secrets, like roots of strange trees.
I ask him the meaning of all that I see,
He grins and he hops, saying, "Just chase me!"

Through fields made of candy and skies full of glitz,
With each sugar rush, laughter endlessly flits.
The clock strikes a chime, time's playing a game,
Each moment so fleeting, but none is the same.

So I jump into colors, mix blue with the pink,
Pour puddles of giggles in ink where I think.
With dreams that are dodging, I won't let them go,
In pursuit of the fleeting, the joy starts to grow.

The Glimmer of Unheld Promises

Once I saw a wink from a bright shooting star,
It promised a fortune, but forgot where you are.
Like socks in a dryer, it spun all around,
Leaving whispers of wishes that never were found.

A genie with hiccups, he grants wish askew,
Says, "I'll make you rich, or just give you a shoe!"
I laugh and I ponder the odds of the quest,
Like fishing for jokes in a carnival jest.

A riddle wrapped in riddles, a puzzle with flair,
Unfolding its layers, I'm convinced it's a dare.
To seek out the secrets, the shimmering mirth,
In a world filled with shadows, I search for my worth.

So here's to the sparkle, the glimmering tease,
To promises broken, but made with such ease.
With chuckles and cheers, let's embrace the unknown,
In the dance of the daring, we'll never be alone.

A Glance Beyond the Horizon

Beyond the tall mountains, I peek and I pry,
Where clouds wear their hats, and the sun goes awry.
A penguin named Percy plays frisbee with fate,
While chickens play peek-a-boo, isn't it great?

A breeze whispers gently, it teases my hair,
As I stumble on questions that float everywhere.
I search for a map, but the paths twist and bend,
With each silly turn, I discover a friend.

The horizon grins back, it knows all my tricks,
Like juggling pineapples or diving for ticks.
And laughter erupts as I chase after sun,
For every new venture, there's always more fun.

So let's dance on the edge, where the wild dreams play,
With smiles that light up even the dullest of days.
In this curious journey, we'll stumble and shout,
For a glance is just laughter, with joy all about!

The Whispering Winds of Change

A gust of breeze, it calls my name,
Twirling leaves in a wild game.
What's next, a jester or a fool?
Oh look, a chicken swims in a pool!

Each turn I take, a surprise awaits,
Clowns and puppies, and jumping gates.
Sunshine dances, shadows play,
What's the lesson? I've lost my way!

Whispers tease the quiet night,
A squirrel debates its next big flight.
Time ticks on with a winky glance,
Will I laugh or might I prance?

In this circus, I wonder why,
I chase the clouds, the stars, the sky.
So join the dance, embrace the weird,
In curiosity, my heart is steered.

Intrigued by Tomorrow

Tomorrow's promise, a silly tease,
What will burst forth, a pop or wheeze?
A dancing taco might take the stage,
The thought alone sparks my inner rage!

Will I find gold or just a shoe?
The world's a mess with a funny view.
Perhaps I'll stumble on a nugget bright,
Or watch a cat do a backflip in flight.

Each dawn breaks with zany flair,
What if the sun wore purple hair?
Tomorrow's riddle wrapped in delight,
Let's jump on puddles, oh what a sight!

With speculation spilling from my cup,
I can't wait to see what will erupt.
So bring on the clowns, or maybe a mime,
Every day's a ruckus—let's throw in some rhyme!

The Flicker of What Might Be

Flickering thoughts, what might they show?
A pig in a hat? A cat with a bow?
Oh, the wonders tied in a flicker bright,
Why did the chicken cross? I want that insight!

With puzzles jumbled like socks in a dryer,
Each twist and turn fuels my desire.
Maybe I'll meet a talking fish,
Or a flying elephant, oh, what a wish!

In the realm of maybes and dreams galore,
A sandwich speaks, 'Don't forget to explore!'
Every twist, a giggle, every turn, a grin,
In the dance of fate, where do I begin?

So toast to the flicker, let's raise our cheer,
To the zany adventures that always appear.
With whimsy untold and mischief at bay,
I'll keep guessing, come what may!

The Curiosity of Being

Curiosity blooms in this odd parade,
A turtle jogging or a fish that swayed?
Oh, the antics of whimsy in endless supply,
I can't help but ponder, oh my, oh my!

Each day's an riddle wrapped in delight,
Is that a bird or a plane in flight?
Perhaps a dragon in a top hat and cane,
Who knows what strange changes will entertain?

With questions a-plenty, I simply shall roam,
In this quirky cosmos, I truly feel at home.
So where's the compass in spiraled confounds?
Let's follow the giggles and chase silly sounds!

In this whimsically wild, swirling dance,
I'll twirl and I'll leap and invite my chance.
For in every odd thing, there lies a thrill,
What fun it is to just wonder and chill!

Uncharted Waters of Thought

In a sea of thoughts, I float around,
A fish with ideas, not yet drowned.
I cast my net for wisdom, oh dear,
But catch a shoe and a rubber duck, oh dear!

With every wave, a riddle pops,
Like trying to find where my pen always hops.
I search for answers with diligent glee,
Only to find my lunch and a lost key!

Curious currents pull me along,
Is that a seagull, or just my song?
I chase the tide, embrace the whirl,
In this wild ocean, I twirl and swirl.

Maybe the treasure's not gold or fame,
But a smile that sparkles like a wild game.
So I'll sail this madness, never be still,
For each twist and turn is a laugh, what a thrill!

When Expectation Meets Surprise

Got a plan, it's well-defined,
Then the toaster burns and I'm re-tined.
That bread was supposed to toast well,
Now it's a charred story I must tell!

Hopes were high for a sunny day,
But rainclouds come to join the fray.
Instead of puddles, I find my shoes,
Squishing and sloshing in my merry blues!

Expect to dance, but trip on a sock,
Life's little quirks around the clock.
It's a sitcom played out in real time,
With slapstick moments, we laugh and mime.

When plans go sideways, don't pout or frown,
Just wear a smile, drop that crown!
In the chaos, find the fun,
It's a show where no one's outdone!

The Intrigue of Everyday Moments

A coffee spill, the cat on the floor,
Who knew a nap could lead to a war?
With each little blunder, a chuckle ignites,
As I wrestle my thoughts in the quiet nights.

Lost my keys in the fridge again,
Might as well check for a chicken pen!
The mundane is magic, quirky and spry,
In the drama of life, I laugh and cry.

Yesterday's groceries turn into jest,
Who knew life could so heavily jest?
A sock on my foot, the other on Mars,
Swirling in laughter beneath the stars.

Every detail has stories to share,
Like mismatched socks or the stain in my chair.
The intrigue is constant, a game without end,
In the riddle of days, we bend and transcend!

Beyond the Horizon's Edge

Set my sights on what lies ahead,
Beyond this hill, where dreams are bred.
Each morning whispers, what could be,
As I chase the sun like a bumblebee!

Rumors of gold at the rainbow's end,
But all I find is that silly trend.
A unicorn made of pancake mix,
Or a field of flowers that dance and fix!

With each step forward, doubts percolate,
Will I stumble, or will I elate?
But the jest in the journey steals the show,
As I trip over nothing, down I go!

So on I wander, with giggles as guides,
To places unknown, where oddity abides.
Beyond horizons, the laughter extends,
In the wild maze of life, curiosity bends!

The Constant Bending

My plans are like spaghetti, all twirly and bent,
Each fork in the road, a new monster to confront.
With maps that don't line up, I wander with glee,
Do I turn left for joy or right for calamity?

With every choice made, I'm left to reflect,
Is this a great journey or a train wreck defect?
The compass spins wildly, like it's playing a game,
Yet somehow I smile, though nothing's the same.

The calendar's shifty, it's laughing at me,
I plan out my week, but it's always "Gee whiz!"
What I thought was a Monday, was actually a Friday,
How can time be this sneaky? I suppose that's the quiz.

So here I continue, with a grin on my face,
Embracing each twist, at a whimsical pace.
The bends and the curves are my silly old friends,
And I'll ride this wild rollercoaster 'til it ends.

A Quest for the Unexpected

I set out on a journey, oh what a grand quest,
In search of bizarre snacks, what could be the best?
A taco in a cupcake, or sushi with jam,
Adventure's afoot, Oh wow, look at that clam!

I sail through the markets, oh what will I find?
Pickles in a pie? Who's crafting this kind?
Each corner I turn, yields more kooky delights,
My taste buds are dancing, they're outrageous tonight!

The list keeps on growing, a smorgasbord feast,
From donuts with bacon to pickles, at least!
But as I dig in, the surprise hits my tongue,
The flavor's a puzzle; it's got me uphung!

Yet, here I am smiling, with snacks all around,
For every odd bite, there's joy to be found.
Unexpected delights are the spice of this life,
So let's munch together, and banish the strife!

The Dance of Intrigue

In the ballroom of ploys, where whimsies take flight,
I dance with my doubts, oh what a strange sight!
My partner is chaos, he twirls me around,
With steps like a puzzle, we leap and we bound.

With every misstep, I chuckle and sway,
The rules aren't for dancing, we'll make it our way!
A shimmy to the left, and a slide to the right,
Here comes the boogie that'll last through the night.

Oh la la, what a tango; my feet are confused,
With moves that don't follow, yet I'm not overly bruised.
For laughter is leading this unpredictable spree,
In the dance of intrigue, we're wildly carefree!

So twirl all you want, let the music enthrall,
We'll tango through life, and we'll never fall.
For the joy's in the dance, with all of its strange,
Even if my two left feet are planning to change.

Navigating Life's Labyrinth

Here I stand in a maze, with walls made of cheese,
A snack for the journey, oh how I feel pleased!
But wait, there's a hedgehog, with clues and a riddle,
He leads me in circles while I munch on a twiddle.

Each turn that I take, stirs laughter or fright,
A shortcut to nowhere, or a door that's just bright?
A goblin appears, with a map drawn in crayon,
He says 'Follow this path, but I'm not really stayin'.

The minotaur's snoring, he's napping away,
Should I sneak by the snorer, or join in the play?
In this wacky old fortress, what more can I say?
The labyrinth's full of giggles, come laugh as we sway.

So I'll frolic through puzzles, with cheese cubes for snacks,
Gathering giggles while I follow the tracks.
With surprises at each corner, I'll dance through this game,
For navigating this maze is the fun part, just the same!

In Search of the Elusive Spark

In a world full of quirky things,
I chase a spark like it has wings.
It winks and giggles, then runs away,
Leaving me puzzled at the end of the day.

I ask a squirrel, he shrugs and scampers,
A cantankerous cat, he just laughs and tamper.
I wonder if I'm the punchline of fate,
The spark's a tease, always running late.

I chase it in circles, my coffee's gone cold,
I try to get wise, but the cosmos is bold.
So I dance with shadows, twirl with the breeze,
Laughing at life's many funny unease.

If tomorrow arrives with a grand surprise,
I'll open my arms and embrace the skies.
For in this chase, joy reigns supreme,
Even if the spark remains a dream.

The Layers of Wonder

I peel back layers like an onion's skin,
Searching for joy, where to begin?
Each layer unveiled, I meet something new,
A dancing potato that says 'How do you do?'

Underneath it all, there lies a prank,
A rubber chicken in a deep sea tank.
Each bite of mystery tastes strange yet sweet,
Am I tasting spices, or just my own feet?

I ponder existence with a slice of pie,
Wondering if ducks really do fly high.
A zingy zing here, a zesty zazz there,
My brain's on a ride, but does it care?

As I laugh through the layers, deep down I find,
A treasure of chuckles, a jester unlined.
The world is a stage, of marshmallows and glee,
With every layer peeled, more fun awaits me.

Between the Known and Unknown

What's hiding in the canyon of the gray?
Is it a gnome with a flute, or a cat that can play?
I ride the line where questions balance right,
With a taco in one hand, feeling quite light.

Between the known and the crazy surprise,
A llama in a tutu just winks at my eyes.
I toss out my queries like confetti in air,
Will the answer come back, or is it just flair?

The unknown dances wildly, with confound and twist,
Like ordering coffee and getting a tryst.
I sit on a teeter, like a seesaw of fate,
Wondering if mysteries work on a date.

Yet that's where the magic and laughter unfurl,
In feedback loops that twist and swirl.
So here I will stand, between laughter and frown,
With a pizza slice high, I ain't backing down!

The Spectrum of Possibility

In the wild expanse of colors so bright,
I tickle a rainbow, oh what a sight!
With hues full of mischief and glee all around,
Possibilities sprout like confetti unbound.

A pink giraffe prances with plaid-tied flair,
Could this be a dream or a whim in the air?
Sorting through scenarios as silly as pie,
I wonder if chickens could teach me to fly?

The spectrum throws shadows, both sharp and meek,
I chuckle at choices and curiosity's peak.
Every moment's a tickle, a jest in disguise,
Where questions dance playfully, beneath the blue skies.

So, let's grapple our dreams with a wink and a grin,
For in the absurd, life truly begins.
With laughter my compass, I won't skip a beat,
Exploring the colors, life's sometimes odd treat.

Echoes of Uncertainty

Why did the chicken cross the street?
To find a treat, not admit defeat!
A sock in the dryer, a mystery's call,
Is it wedged in a chair or trapped in a ball?

The cat looks wise with a twitch of his tail,
Plotting a scheme, will he succeed or fail?
Each morning's a riddle, come join the quest,
What's for breakfast? A cereal fest?

Wobbly tables spin thoughts so bizarre,
Is there a purpose or just a quasar?
In the circus of life, we juggle our fears,
With laughter and chaos, while downing our beers.

The answer to nothing is all that we know,
A dance through confusion, come join the show!
With echoes of life teasing clarify,
You'll never guess it; just eat your pie!

Chasing Shadows of Destiny

My fortune cookie said to chase the sun,
But it didn't mention I'd fried up my bun!
In pursuit of a goal, I tripped on my feet,
The shadows they giggled, oh what a feat!

A rabbit that pauses like it's on a break,
Hops through my window, for goodness' sake!
What's in that hat? Gold coins or a shoe?
Maybe it's magic, or just a big stew.

Wiggly worms wiggle like they've lost the race,
Searching for wisdom, a cosmic embrace.
With laughter as fuel, we dance down the lane,
Even the rain joins in with its refrain.

Chasing elusive, those shadows slide by,
As I tumble and giggle, I can't help but sigh.
The path may be twisted, but what do I know?
Follow the laughs, let them steal the show!

The Game of Serendipity

Roll the dice, but don't take a peek,
Could be a fortune or just a leak!
I wore mismatched socks to shake up the fate,
And my fortune teller laughed, "Oh, that's just great!"

Found a penny and wished for a snack,
But it led me to dance with a curious quack.
With ducks as my partners in awkward ballet,
The universe chuckles, "What a fine day!"

A key to the treasure? Or just a good joke?
In this game of mischief, predictably broke.
With every wrong turn, there's glitter and glee,
Serendipity whispers, "Hey, dance with me!"

Every door that is closed opens a new,
With pie in the oven, and laughs that ensue.
So spin like a top in a whirl of delight,
In the game of the curious, everything's bright!

Questions Beneath the Stars

Why do birds sing at the break of the dawn?
Is it a secret? Or just a ploy gone wrong?
Under twinkling stars, where wonders collide,
I ponder the mysteries the night tries to hide.

Where's my missing sock? Is it lost in space?
Did it soar to the moon or disguise as a vase?
Stars twinkle brightly, in jest I can see,
That chaos is cozy, just wild and free!

With quirky thoughts bouncing, the cosmos awake,
Should I trust my instincts or take a big break?
The questions are plenty, but answers are few,
Like trying to find where the wild daisies grew.

So dance with the queries that float through the night,
Embrace every riddle, every laugh, every plight!
For beneath all the stars, we're all just a guess,
In a cosmos of laughter, we find our real mess!

Flickers of Fate

A sock is lost, the toaster smokes,
A cat gives side-eye, it just provokes.
I trip on thoughts, like shoelaces undone,
What's the secret? Is it meant for fun?

I chase my dreams like ice cream cones,
They melt away while I'm on my phone.
A twist of fate in every bite,
Each creamy scoop brings planned delight.

Life's riddles dance in a spinny chair,
A leap of faith? Or just a dare?
I wear mismatched socks, it feels so right,
Are they just clues to a peculiar night?

As laughter echoes through parks and lanes,
Each chuckle hints at silly refrains.
All in good fun, let's play this game,
For every twist, we can stake our claim.

Questions in the Wind

Why is cereal round, yet milk is square?
Do penguins waddle or just really care?
Clouds tease with shapes, a dragon, a hat,
Are we all just puppets? Or cats?

Oh, where do socks go when they disappear?
It's a mystery equal to human cheer.
Ghosts in my fridge, do they eat my cheese?
Why do I fall for a cat with a sneeze?

I ask the stars if they know the score,
But they just twinkle and shine some more.
Each question floats like a hired kite,
Do answers dance or just take flight?

So here's to wonders, like bubbles in drinks,
With giggles and grins, let's swirl and think.
Curiosity is the spark that ignites,
In this wild world, let's embrace the sights.

The Enigma Within Us

I wear my quirks like a hat on a bird,
Flapping about, it's totally absurd.
Why do I trip but never quite fall?
Maybe it's fate, or just life's silly call.

Puzzles of jellybeans spin in my mind,
Each color a choice, what joy I find!
A riddle wrapped in a mystery coat,
Is that a whisper or just my throat?

I ask a mirror, "What's the right way?"
It just reflects back with a grin in play.
Is the answer hidden in silly mistakes?
Or do we just giggle, and that's what it takes?

So let's toast to inquiries, both big and small,
For every giggle, one day we'll recall.
Underneath chaos, we'll find the sweet hub,
Life's quirky path — a fabulous rub.

Journeys Without Maps

Lost on a road where no signs exist,
I follow a squirrel, can't resist!
It twitches its tail, a fine guide indeed,
For missing my turn, sometimes we lead.

Google says left, but I went right,
So here I am, in the moonlight!
A twisty trail of laughter and fear,
Every wrong move, I cheer, "Yay! Here!"

My compass spins like a top in the air,
Is it leading me somewhere rare?
A path with marshmallows or rivers of cheese,
Let's skip along in the playful breeze!

So here's to the journeys that stray from the track,
If we trip and we tumble, there's no looking back.
With quirky companions, our hearts will map,
In the chaos and giggles, we'll always find zap!

The Unfolding Mystery

I woke up with a grand plan in mind,
But my socks just refused to be matched.
My breakfast was cereal, the milk poured out fast,
While the spoon staged a slip; how had it attached?

I strolled to the office in mismatched shoes,
Even my coffee was temperamental, too.
A client walked in with a chicken for shock,
Guess I'd worry about tight budgets anew!

The agenda was set, but my pen ran dry,
As I scribbled my notes, it wrote 'I love pie!'
But amidst all the chaos, there's joy in the rush,
Every twist and turn brings a reason to hush.

So I'll dance through the day with this lighthearted glee,
With the weird little wonders that life sends to me.
At the end of the riddle, perhaps true surprise,
Is the laughter that echoes in unexpected skies.

Echoes of Hidden Pathways

In the maze of my thoughts, I took a wrong turn,
The signs all pointed, but they looked like they burned.
I ran into a rabbit in a top hat and suit,
He said, "You're late for the tea too! Don't dispute!"

Every corner I turned, a new puzzle appears,
With a gadget that squeaks and a duck that just cheers.
"Waddling through life," the wise fowl exclaimed,
"It's the quirky and odd that keep us well-trained!"

A fork in the road, which one should I take?
One leads to the cake, the other to the lake.
I chose the sweet slice, with icing galore,
But the ducks were not happy, they quacked for more!

Yet hidden's the beauty in winding our ways,
With laughter and whimsy to brighten our days.
So cheers to the chaos and puzzles anew,
Where every surprise breeds a chuckle or two.

An Odyssey of Surprises

Packed up my bags, set out with delight,
Only to find my suitcase was light.
No clothes, just a lizard and half of a shoe,
But they both told me fun's just waiting for you!

A taxi appeared, it was purple and small,
The driver was juggling, I laughed through it all.
"Where to, my friend?" he did ask with a grin,
"To the land of the weird, let the madness begin!"

The airport was bustling with flamingo pals,
Reciting their poetry from paper thin salves.
I joined in the fun, won a prize for my style,
Turns out, embarrassing? That's just my own smile!

As the adventure unfolded with joy in each step,
I learned that in oddness, my heart's depth is kept.
So here's to surprises and stories we weave,
In the rush of the day, it's the laughter we leave.

The Unpredictable Brevity

One moment I'm planning a trip to the stars,
The next I'm stuck getting ice cream at bars.
With choices like popcorn, or cake to devour,
Time flies while I ponder the best way to shower!

With clocks that are melting like some dreams do,
I chased after time, it said, "Try the stew!"
"Why stew?" I inquired, with a raised eyebrow,
It chuckled, then slipped on a banana peel how!

A quick glance at the clock, it winked with a cheer,
I asked for directions, it just said "Stay here."
So I twirled with my thoughts, a dance full of glee,
What's clearer than chaos is just being free!

In the end, I conclude with a giggle and grin,
It's the brief moments of joy where the fun can begin.
So here's to the fleeting and odd of the day,
May they linger in laughter, and never decay.

www.ingramcontent.com/pod-product-compliance
Lightning Source LLC
Chambersburg PA
CBHW051637160426
43209CB00004B/692